When the Sun Goes Down

Mick Manning
and Brita Granström

W
FRANKLIN WATTS
LONDON·SYDNEY

For Jan-Erik Granström

First published in 2001
by Franklin Watts,
96 Leonard Street,
London EC2A 4XD

Franklin Watts Australia
56 O'Riordan Street
Alexandria
NSW 2015

The illustrations in this book have been drawn
by both Mick and Brita

Text and illustrations © 2001 Mick Manning
and Brita Granström
Series editor: Rachel Cooke
Art director: Jonathan Hair

Printed in Hong Kong, China
A CIP catalogue record is available from
the British Library.
Dewey Classification 529
ISBN 0 7496 4179 7

Contents

Goodnight

When the sun goes
down, it gets dark.
It's our bedtime.
But out there,
in the night . . .

At sunset, it's not the sun
moving but the earth!
As the earth turns, the
part facing away from
the sun becomes dark.

Night-time animals
Foxes chase their prey.

Foxes hunt rabbits, worms and
small animals like mice and rats.

Foxes that live in towns are called urban
foxes. They steal food from dustbins, too. 9

Animals active at
night are called
nocturnal animals.

Owls have excellent
hearing and eyesight
for hunting at night.

Owls hunt over fields.

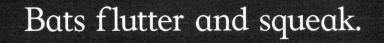

Bats flutter and squeak.

A bat's high-pitched squeaks
echo off objects in their path.
When it hears the echo,
the bat can tell where
things are in the dark –
including the insects it eats.

Cats prowl through
the shadows . . .

Cats use their
whiskers as well as
their eyes and ears
to find their prey.

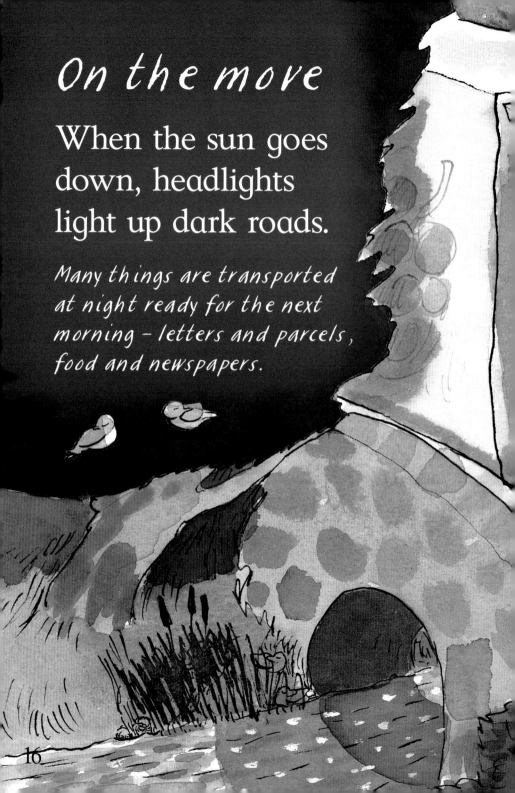

On the move

When the sun goes down, headlights light up dark roads.

Many things are transported at night ready for the next morning – letters and parcels, food and newspapers.

Glass cats' eyes shine in the middle of the road. They reflect the lights from cars and trucks.

Far away
from the city lights,
bright stars crowd the sky.

*Far, far away in space there are other suns
– the stars – and shining planets, too.
To see them clearly, you need to have
very few electric lights around.*

19

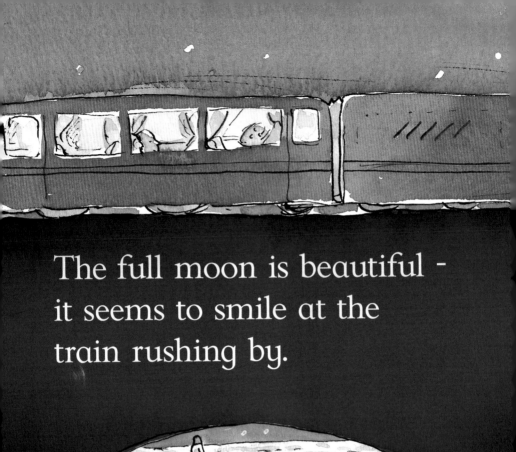

The full moon is beautiful -
it seems to smile at the
train rushing by.

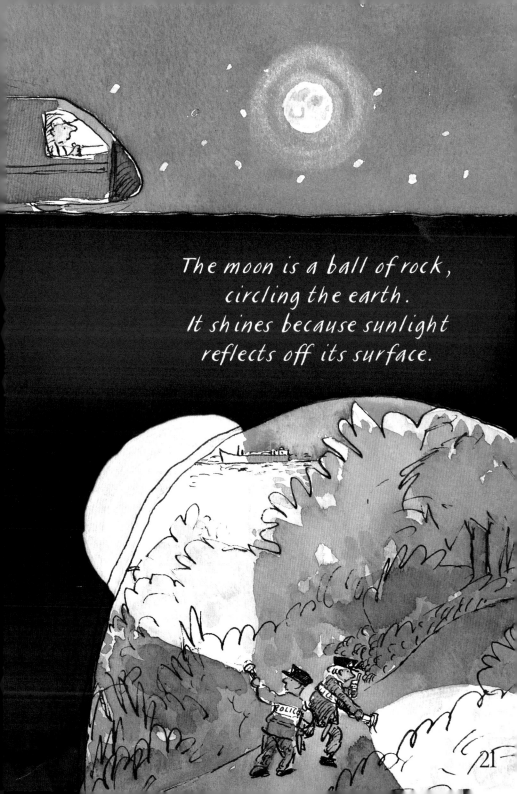

The moon is a ball of rock,
circling the earth.
It shines because sunlight
reflects off its surface.

Working hard

Nightshifts 'clock on'.
People unload lorries
and stack shelves.

The police are on patrol.

Bakers are baking.
Postal workers sort
letters and parcels.

24

A street sweeper
is tidying the street,
ready for tomorrow.

Good-morning

Listen to the dawn chorus! The sun is rising - it's starting to get light. Letters 'plop' on the doormat. Wake up sleepyheads - it's daytime again!

Birds sing their 'dawn chorus' in the spring and summer just before the sun rises. Have you ever heard it?

Night-time ideas

Find out more about what happens while you are asleep.

The turning earth

Our earth is shaped like a ball, spinning in space. As it turns, it's daytime on the side that faces the sun and night-time on the side facing away.

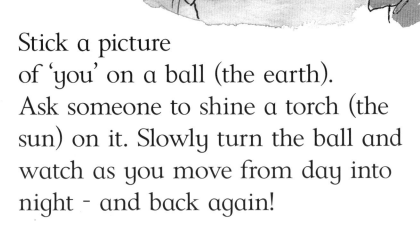

Stick a picture of 'you' on a ball (the earth). Ask someone to shine a torch (the sun) on it. Slowly turn the ball and watch as you move from day into night - and back again!

Animal senses

Night-time animals use all their senses to find their food - not just their eyes. Hide some fruit with a strong smell - like bananas - in your room. Close the curtains and see if your friends can find the fruit - using all their senses!

Moon chart

The moon looks a little different each night. Over 28 days, it waxes (grows bigger) and then wanes (grows smaller).

Draw 28 circles on a chart. Over 28 nights, fill in each circle with the moon's shape - when you can see it!

Night words and index